ANIMAL BABIES

BABY KOALAS

by Jenna Grodzicki

Consultant: Beth Gambro
Reading Specialist, Yorkville, Illinois

BEARPORT PUBLISHING

Minneapolis, Minnesota

Teaching Tips

Before Reading

- Look at the cover of the book. Discuss the picture and the title.
- Ask readers to brainstorm a list of what they already know about koalas. What can they expect to see in this book?
- Go on a picture walk, looking through the pictures to discuss vocabulary and make predictions about the text.

During Reading

- Read for purpose. Encourage readers to think about koalas and the animal life cycle as they are reading.
- If readers encounter an unknown word, ask them to look at the sounds in the word. Then, ask them to look at the rest of the page. Are there any clues to help them understand?

After Reading

- Encourage readers to pick a buddy and reread the book together.
- Ask readers to name three things that koalas do between the time they are born and when they are ready to have babies. Go back and find the pages that tell about these things.
- Ask readers to write a sentence and draw a picture of something that they learned about koalas.

Credits:
Cover and title page, © Andras Deak/Shutterstock; 3, © Eric Isselee/Shutterstock; 5, © Roland Seitre/Minden Pictures; 6, © mayakova/Shutterstock and © D. Parer and E. Parer-Cook/Minden Pictures; 7, © stelioskyriakides/iStock; 9, © Ian Waldie/Getty Images; 10, © blickwinkel/Alamy Stock Photo; 13, © EQRoy/Alamy Stock Photo; 15, © Freder/iStock; 16, © TonyFeder/iStock; 19, © Maurizio De Mattei/Shutterstock; 20, © asiafoto/iStock; 22, © Andras Deak/Shutterstock; 23BR, © blickwinkel/Alamy Stock Photo; 23BL, © EQRoy/Alamy Stock Photo; 23TL, © Suzi Eszterhas/Minden Pictures; 23TR, © CraigRJD/iStock

Library of Congress Cataloging-in-Publication Data

Names: Grodzicki, Jenna, 1979– author.
Title: Baby koalas / Jenna Grodzicki.
Description: Bearcub books edition. | Minneapolis, Minnesota : Bearport
Publishing Company, [2021] | Series: Animal babies | Includes bibliographical references and index.
Identifiers: LCCN 2020038310 (print) | LCCN 2020038311 (ebook) | ISBN
9781647474706 (library binding) | ISBN 9781647474782 (paperback) | ISBN
9781647474867 (ebook)
Subjects: LCSH: Koala—Infancy—Juvenile literature.
Classification: LCC QL737.M384 G78 2021 (print) | LCC QL737 .M384 (ebook)
| DDC 599.2/5—dc23
LC record available at https://lccn.loc.gov/2020038310
LC ebook record available at https://lccn.loc.gov/2020038311

For more information, write to Bearport Publishing, 5357 Penn Avenue South, Minneapolis, MN 55419.

Printed in the United States of America.

Contents

It's a Baby Koala!

A mother koala just had a baby.

The baby can't see or hear.

But it can smell.

It sniffs its way to its mother's **pouch**.

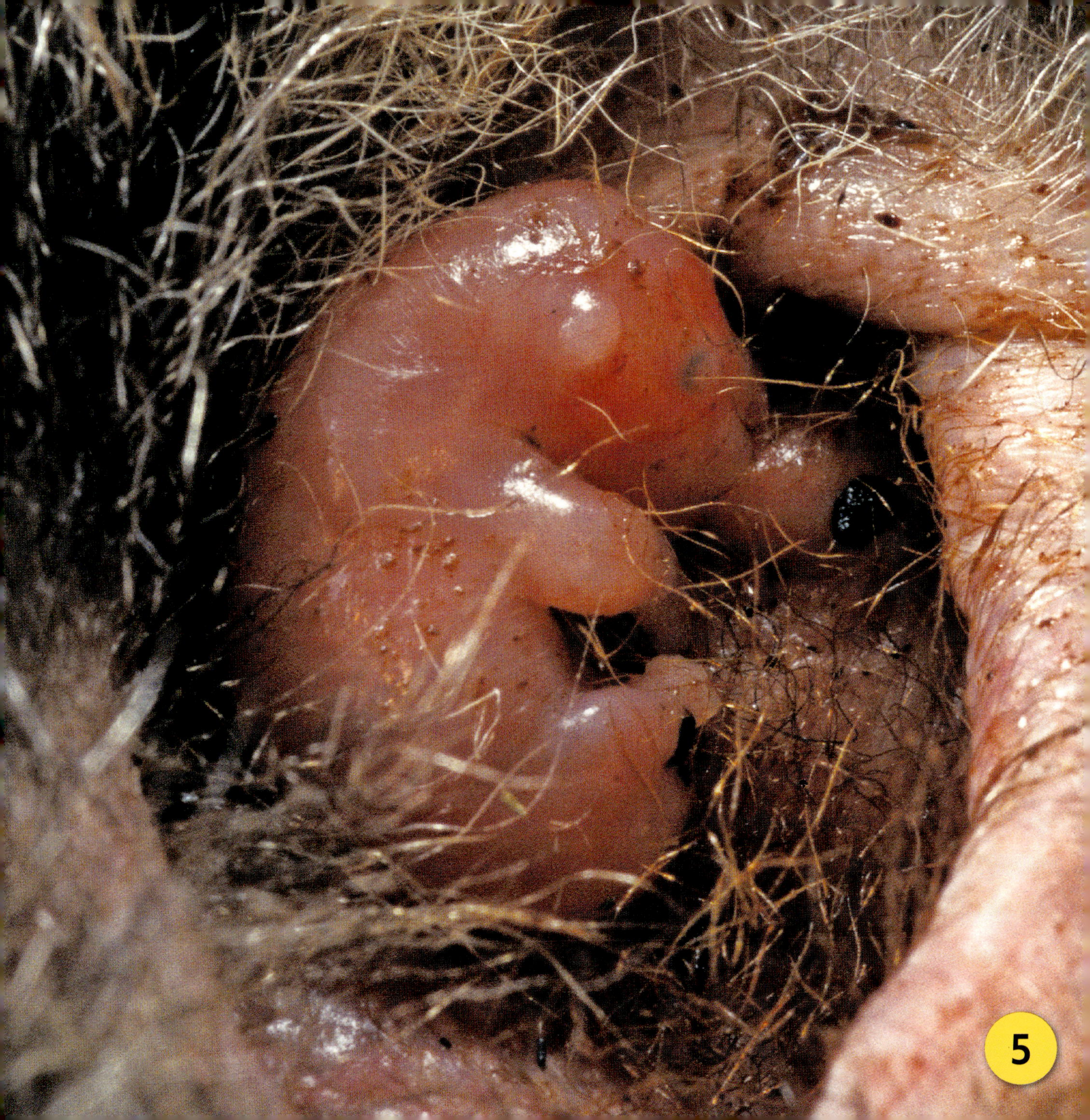

The baby is very small.

It is the size of a jelly bean.

The little koala stays safe in the pouch.

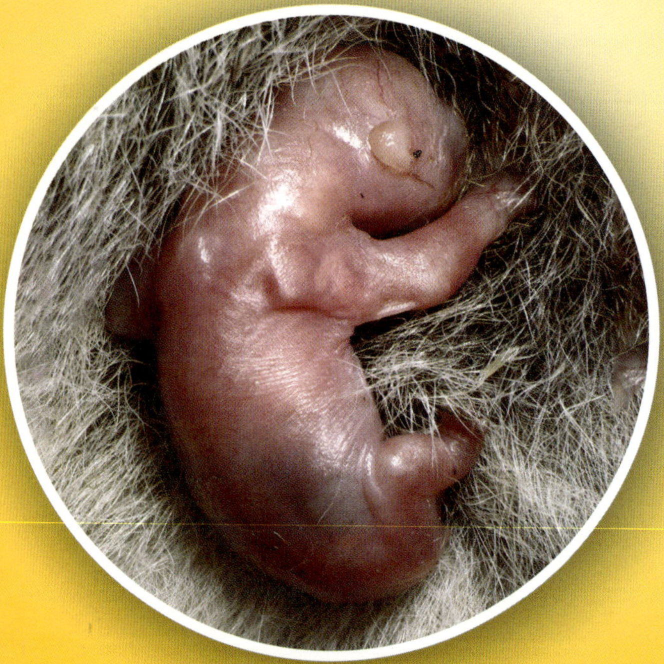

The baby
is in here.

A baby koala is called a **joey**.

The joey drinks milk from its mother's body.

Milk helps it grow.

After five months, the joey opens its eyes.

It pokes its head out of the pouch.

Peekaboo!

Soon, the mother makes something new for the joey.

It is called **pap**.

Pap is a kind of koala poop.

The joey eats it!

Yum!

The joey begins to go out of the pouch for short trips.

It holds onto its mother's back.

Time for a ride!

The joey starts to eat leaves, too.

It picks the new food with its paws.

It still crawls back into the pouch to drink and sleep.

Soon, the joey spends some time away from its mother.

It learns to **climb**.

Be careful!

When the koala is a year old, it goes on its own.

It grows for another year or two.

Then, the koala can have babies.

The Baby's Body

Glossary

climb to move up or down, such as in a tree

joey a baby animal, such as a koala

pap wet poop a mother koala makes for the joey to eat

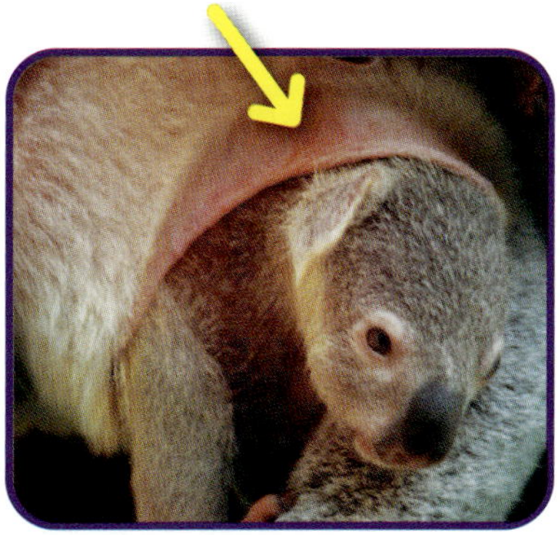

pouch a part of a mother koala's belly used to hold and carry a baby

Index

Read More

Fishman, Jon M. *Meet a Baby Koala (Baby Australian Animals).* Minneapolis: Lerner Publications, 2018.

Murray, Julie. *Koala Joeys (Baby Animals).* Minneapolis: Abdo Kids, 2018.

Learn More Online

1. Go to **www.factsurfer.com**
2. Enter "**Baby Koalas**" into the search box.
3. Click on the cover of this book to see a list of websites.

About the Author

Jenna Grodzicki loves to read and go to the beach with her husband and two children.